THE BOOK OF QUALITIES

THE·BOOK OF·QUALITIES

words and pictures by

J·RUTH GENDLER

PERENNIAL LIBRARY

Harper & Row, Publishers, New York
Cambridge, Philadelphia, San Francisco, Washington
London, Mexico City, São Paulo, Singapore, Sydney

The Book of Qualities was originally published in 1984 by Turquoise Mountain Publi-
cations.

First PERENNIAL LIBRARY edition published 1988.

LIBRARY OF CONGRESS CATALOG CARD NUMBER: 87-45617
ISBN: 0-06-096252-6

88   89   90   91   92   MPC   10   9   8   7   6   5   4   3   2   1

to my parents

THE QUALITIES

the Wind

The Wind is a gossip. Not in a malicious way. She just likes to move around and stir things up. She runs through the fire barefoot and has no fear of heights. She carries big blue bowls of rain with her. She plays the flute and loves all kinds of sounds. Her laughter fills the sky. The Wind is a wonderful story-teller. I still remember how she introduced me to the Qualities when I was a child.

Pleasure

Pleasure is wild and sweet. She likes purple flowers. She loves the sun and the wind and the night sky. She carries a silver bowl full of liquid moonlight. She has a cat named Midnight with stars on his paws.

Many people mistrust Pleasure, and even more misunderstand her. For a long time I could hardly stand to be in the same room with her. I went to sleep early to avoid her. I thought she was a gossip and a flirt and she drank too much. In school we learned that she was dangerous, and I was sure that she would distract me from my work. I didn't realize she could nurture me.

As I have changed, Pleasure has changed. I have learned to value her friendship.

Worry

Worry has written the definitive work on nervous habits. She etches lines on people's foreheads when they are not paying attention. She makes lists of everything that could go wrong while she is waiting for the train. She is sure she left the stove on, and the house is going to explode in her absence. When she makes love, her mind is on the failure rates and health hazards of various methods of birth control. The drug companies want Worry to test their new tranquilizers but they don't understand what she knows too well: there is no drug that can ease her pain. She is terrified of the unknown.

Fear

Fear has a large shadow, but he himself is quite small. He has a vivid imagination. He composes horror music in the middle of the night. He is not very social, and he keeps to himself at political meetings. His past is a mystery. He warned us not to talk to each other about him, adding that there is nowhere any of us could go where he wouldn't hear us. We were quiet. When we began to talk to each other, he changed. His manners started to seem pompous, and his snarling voice sounded rehearsed.

Two dragons guard Fear's mansion. One is ceramic and Chinese. The other is real. If you make it past the dragons and speak to him close up, it is amazing to see how fragile he is. He will try to tell you stories. Be aware. He is a master of disguises and illusions. Fear almost convinced me that he was a puppet-maker and I was a marionette.

Speak out boldly, look him in the eye, startle him. Don't give up. Win his respect, and he will never bother you with small matters.

Patience

Patience wears my grandmother's filigree earrings. She bakes marvelous dark bread. She has beautiful hands. She carries great sacks of peace and purses filled with small treasures. You don't notice Patience right away in a crowd, but suddenly you see her all at once, and then she is so beautiful you wonder why you never saw her before.

Confusion

When Confusion's parents
separated, neither one of them
wanted him. Each claimed he
most resembled the other. He is a
tall boy, and lately he has gotten
a bit plump. He is always trying
to make people like him. His
attempts usually backfire.

Confusion is very accident-
prone. He lives from crisis to
crisis. Even the clearest
directions are impossible for
him to follow. My friends
shudder when they see
him heading toward their
studios. He is well-meaning,
but not nearly as innocent
as he seems.

Confusion is Patience's
nephew. She is the only one
who can sing to him.

Loneliness

Loneliness loves to run, but he is afraid to swim. He wears his isolation around him like a grey sweatshirt thrown back across the shoulders. It started when he was a little boy listening to the adults upstairs screaming at each other as he hid under the covers. At age seven he vowed never to need anyone. It was as if he sealed himself inside his skin, separate from everyone.

Once Loneliness almost changed his mind. There was a woman whom he cherished. She surprised him. He loved her so much that he thought he would never be himself again. He trusted that such a relationship could not survive, and it didn't. Now more convinced than ever that companionship is a lie and joy is fragile, he has become contemptuous of others' happiness.

Despair

Despair papered her bathroom walls with newspaper articles on acid rain. For years she worked with abused children. She has documented how we all suffer from malnourishment based on insufficient amounts of love. She has investigated how the pain of concentration camp survivors has been transmitted from one generation to the next "through disturbances in the parent/child relationship." Not only the children but the grandchildren and their children.

Despair is overworked and overwhelmed. She has a heart condition. In her dreams the war is everywhere. She is not lying or exaggerating. Still, it is difficult to be around her. There is no arguing with her. She is persuasive, eloquent, and undeniably well-informed. If you attempt to change her mind, you will come away agreeing with her. She has stopped listening to music.

Judgment

Judgment does not like many people, but he loves a few very much. Although he is arrogant, he is not nearly as confident as others assume. He does not quite know how to handle all his insight, so people get the wrong idea. He is not ruthless, but steady and obsessed by his search for the truth.

Discipline

Discipline does not disappear forever, but she does take vacations from time to time. By nature she is a conservative person, and yet she lives a radical life. Guided by a sense of inner necessity, she works hard and takes many risks. When Discipline was a teenager too poor to afford dance classes, she skipped lunch to pay for her lessons.

Discipline has a strong sense of order. However, when things are too neat she feels compelled to mess them up. She has a complex relationship to form. She appreciates the necessity and dangers of structure. She understands that the same structure which supports you can also hold you back. The bones of the skeleton which support the body can become the bars of the cage which imprison the spirit. After Discipline has mastered a form, she is free to improvise.

Courage

Courage has roots. She sleeps on a futon on the floor and lives close to the ground. Courage looks you straight in the eye. She is not impressed with powertrippers, and she knows first aid. Courage is not afraid to weep, and she is not afraid to pray, even when she is not sure who she is praying to. When Courage walks, it is clear that she has made the journey from loneliness to solitude. The people who told me she is stern were not lying; they just forgot to mention that she is kind.

Anxiety

Anxiety is secretive. He does not trust anyone, not even his friends, Worry, Terror, Doubt, and Panic. He has a way of glombing onto your skin like smog, and then you feel unclean. He likes to visit me late at night when I am alone and exhausted. I have never slept with him, but he kissed me on the forehead once, and I had a headache for two years. He is sure a nuisance to get out of the house. He has no respect for locks or curtains or doors. I speak from experience. It takes cunning to get rid of him, a combination of anger, humor, and self-respect. A bath helps too. He does not like to get wet. As a last resort, if you are not near a bathtub, wet your face with tears.

Stillness

Stillness will meet you for tea or a walk by the ocean. You must be gentle when you approach her. She is more sensitive than we can even imagine and she does not explain herself much. Sometimes I bring her flowers — not because she needs them (she tends several gardens) — but because I am better able to meet her when I am carrying flowers. Her favorite time is dawn.

Clarity

My visits to Clarity are soothing now. He never tells me what to think or feel or do but shows me how to find out what I need to know. It was not always like this. I used to visit other people who visited him. Finally, I summoned the courage to call on him myself. I still remember the first time I went to see him. Was I surprised. He lives on a hill in a little house surrounded by wild roses. I went in the living room and sat down in a comfortable chair by the fireplace. There were topographical maps on the walls, and the room was full of stuff, musical instruments and telescopes and globes, geodes and crystals and old Italian tarot decks, two small cats. When I left, he presented me with a sketchbook and told me to draw the same thing every day until the drawing started to speak to me.

Wisdom

Wisdom wears an indigo jacket. She takes long walks in the purple hills at twilight, pausing to meditate at an old temple near the crossroads. She was sick as a young child so she learned to be alone with herself at an early age.

Wisdom has a quiet mind. She likes to think about the edges where things spill into each other and become their opposites. She knows how to look at things inside and out. Sometimes her eyes go out to the thing she is looking at, and sometimes the thing she is looking at enters through her eyes. Questions of time, depth, and balance interest her. She is not looking for answers.

Trust

Trust is the daughter of Truth. She has an objective memory, neither embellishing nor denying the past. She is an ideal confidante — gracious, candid, and discreet. Trust talks to people who need to hear her; she listens to those who need to be heard; she sits quietly with those who are skeptical of words. Her presence is subtle, simple, and undeniable.

Trust rarely buys round-trip tickets because she is never sure how long she will be gone and when she will return. Trust is at home in the desert and the city, with dolphins and tigers, with outlaws, lovers, and saints. When Trust bought her house, she tore out all the internal walls, strengthened the foundation, and rebuilt the door. Trust is not fragile, but she has no need to advertise her strength. She has a gambler's respect for the interplay between luck and skill; she is the mother of Love.

Uncertainty

I have lived with Uncertainty for a long time. I had thought ours would have been a much briefer affair. I had no idea how intimate we'd become until you showed up.

And now you are asking me to leave him, and there are a few things I need to know. Who are you? What are your motives? Can I trust you? Is it really me you want to spend more time with or Uncertainty you yearn to visit?

Confidence

Confidence ignores "No Trespassing" signs. It is as if he doesn't see them. He is an explorer, committed to following his own direction. He studied mathematics in France and still views his life as a series of experiments. The only limits he respects are his own. He is honest and humble and very funny. After all these years, his sister doesn't understand why he still ice skates with Doubt.

Detachment

I must thank you for introducing me to Detachment. Did you know ahead of time we would like each other so much? He is almost as elusive as you are, but he is more reliable. He rarely calls before he comes over. Usually, I am so pleased to see him that I don't object, and I know there is no way to telephone him when he is on the road. He has clear eyes and a sapphire voice. When he sighs, I can see his heart.

Doubt

Doubt camped out in the living room last week. I told him that we had had too many house guests. Doubt doesn't listen. He keeps saying the same thing again and again and again until I completely forget what I am trying to tell him. Doubt is demanding and not very generous, but I appreciate his honesty.

Faith

Faith lives in the same apartment building as Doubt. When Faith was out of town visiting her uncle in the hospital, Doubt fed the cat and watered the asparagus fern. Faith is comfortable with Doubt because she grew up with him. Their mothers are cousins. Faith is not dogmatic about her beliefs like some of her relatives. Her friends fear that Faith is a bit stupid. They whisper that she is naive and she depends on Doubt to protect her from the meanness of life. In fact, it is the other way around. It is Faith who protects Doubt from Cynicism.

Compassion

Compassion wears Saturn's rings on the fingers of her left hand. She is intimate with the life force. She understands the meaning of sacrifice. She is not afraid to die. There is nothing you cannot tell her.

Compassion speaks with a slight accent. She was a vulnerable child, miserable in school, cold, shy, alert to the pain in the eyes of her sturdier classmates. The other kids teased her about being too sentimental, and for a long time she believed them. In ninth grade she was befriended by Courage.

Courage lent Compassion bright sweaters, explained the slang, showed her how to play volleyball, taught her you can love people and not care what they think about you.

In many ways Compassion is still the stranger, neither wonderful, nor terrible, herself, utterly, always.

Guilt

Guilt is the prosecutor who knows how to make every victim feel like the criminal. She follows the scent of doubt and self-hatred to its sources. She will not tell you what you have done wrong. Her silence is brutal. Her disapproval surrounds you in an envelope of cold nameless terror.

Guilt thinks I am hopelessly lazy because I won't work the way she does. Her court cases are scheduled years in advance. She says horrible things about me to the neighbors. In self-defense sometimes I tell people what she says about me before she has the chance. I don't care as much as I did, but I can't pretend I don't care at all.

You may recognize Guilt's footsteps before you see her coming. She limps like a crippled bird. Even though her broken ankle is healing, the wound in her heart has become infected.

Power

Power made me a coat. For a long time I kept it in the back of my closet. I didn't like to wear it much, but I always took good care of it. When I first started wearing it again, it smelled like mothballs. As I wore it more, it started fitting better, and stopped smelling like mothballs.

I was afraid if I wore the coat too much someone would want to take it or else I would accidentally leave it in the dojo dressing room. But it has my name on the label now, and it doesn't really fit anyone else. When people ask me where I found such a becoming garment, I tell them about the tailor, Power, who knows how to make coats that you grow into. First, you must find the courage to approach him and ask him to make your coat. Then, you must find the patience inside yourself to wear the coat until it fits.

Beauty

Beauty is startling. She wears a gold shawl in the summer and sells seven kinds of honey at the flea market. She is young and old at once, my daughter and my grandmother. In school she excelled in mathematics and poetry. Beauty doesn't anger easily, but she was annoyed with the journalist who kept asking her about her favorites — as if she could have one favorite color or one favorite flower. She does not mind questions though, and she is fond of riddles. Beauty will dance with anyone who is brave enough to ask her.

Criticism

Criticism was always the shortest kid in the class. He learned early to use words to defend himself. As a teenager, Criticism loved to take things apart. At that time he didn't care if they ever got put back together. He retains a strong curiosity about how things work and a deep respect for tools. Criticism is a strict father. He adores his children, but he fears their spontaneity.

Sometimes I want to write Criticism a letter and tell him to leave me alone. The problem is that when I don't see him for a while, I start to miss him. Still, my conversations with him often make me nervous. I usually believe the bad things he says and forget about the good stuff. When we really disagree, I am upset for days and run around asking everyone I meet to reassure me. If I could trust him more, it would be different, but he changes his mind as much as I do. For all his sensitivity, it was years before he realized that other people also have feelings.

When Criticism looks at a painting, he sees the finished picture framed on the wall, and at the same time he sees the picture as it was being painted — what was drawn first, what went in last, where the artist hesitated, where the artist smiled. After Criticism lost his glasses, he discovered that he did not need them anymore. His focus is less acute, but he can see the whole picture better. The colors are more distinct when the outlines are blurred.

You can count on Criticism to have an opinion about everything. He is exceptionally well-read and usually knows what he is talking about. I don't recommend that you speak to him when your project is in the beginning stages. However, as it approaches completion, he can be quite helpful. He is not interested in measuring what you or I do in relationship to each other or anyone else in our fields. At his best, he surveys the distance between our intentions and our accomplishments, between what we are and what we could be.

Perfection

Perfection is careful but not cautious. She burned her hands many times before she learned to pay attention. She says that hers is the most difficult job in the world. The post was vacant for nearly three years. Most people do not even make it past the first interview, and retirement is mandatory after nine years. About halfway through the fifth year Perfection started feeling like she was falling apart and dissolving into space. This recent episode humbled her. She had never realized how strongly we resist being broken open. She discovered that her greatest strengths grew out of her strongest weaknesses.

Perfection needs to keep moving. Otherwise she becomes swollen with her obsessions. She has learned to dance into the very center of her fears. She is not impressed by false modesty and the fronts we develop to hide our beauty. She is grieved by how fiercely we hate ourselves and yet refuse to change. She honors our flaws.

Suffering

Suffering teaches philosophy on a part-time basis. She likes the icy days in February when she can stay home from school, make thick soups, and catch up on her reading. With her white skin and dark hair she even looks like winter. She has a slender face and dramatic cheekbones.

Suffering's reputation troubles her. Certain people adore her and talk about her as if knowing her gives them a special status. Other people despise her; when they see her across the aisle at the supermarket, they look the other way. Even though Suffering is considered a formidable instructor, she is actually quite compassionate. She feels lonely around students who dislike her. It is even more painful to be around those who idealize her. She is proud only because she recognizes the value of her lessons.

Change

Change wears my sister's moccasins. He
stays up late and wakes up early. He likes
to come up quietly and kiss me on the
back of the neck when I am at my drawing
table. He wants to amuse people, and it
hurts him when they yell at him. Change
is very musical, but sometimes you
must listen for a long time before you
hear the pattern in his music.

Excitement

Excitement wears orange socks. He understands the language of flames and loves to build fires. He first taught me how to build a fire when I was seventeen. I was young and scared of being burned. Now I am preparing for another visit. This time I am going to open my heart and let the fire inside.

Excitement is a visionary. He is skilled in the art of friendship. He has worked at many jobs . . . electrician, juggler, sign painter, singer, inventor, poet. Excitement has always moved around. As a teenager, he took a room in Anxiety's house, and last winter Patience sheltered him. The Wind taught Excitement how to be two places at once, and they are still very good friends, though they do not spend much time with each other these days. Sometimes when Excitement dances with the Wind, there is lightning in the sky.

Innocence

Innocence talks to old people on the commuter train. Sometimes she talks to herself, sometimes she talks to the man sitting next to her hiding behind the newspaper, sometimes she talks to the window, and sometimes she sings a little song. She tells secrets in between her words, but most people don't think they're secrets because she says them right out. She told me that it takes a lot of sophistication for her to stay innocent. (That was a secret.) Since her affair with Danger, she is not afraid of anything.

Contentment

Contentment has learned how to find out
what she needs to know. Last year
she went on a major housecleaning
spree. First, she stood on her
head until all the extra facts fell
out. Then, she discarded about
half her house. Now, she knows
where every thing comes from —
who dyed the yarn dark green and who
wove the rug and who built the loom, who
made the willow chair, who planted the
apricot trees. She made the turquoise
mugs herself with clay she found
in the hills beyond her house.

When Contentment is sad, she
takes a mud bath or goes to
the mountains until her
lungs are clear. When
she walks through
an unfamiliar neigh-
borhood, she
always makes
friends
with the
local cats.

Intuition

I invited Intuition to stay in my house when my roommates went North. I warned her that I am territorial and I keep the herb jars in alphabetical order. Intuition confessed that she has a "spotty employment record." She was fired from her last job for daydreaming.

When Intuition moved in, she washed all the windows, cleaned out the fireplace, planted fruit trees, and lit purple candles. She doesn't cook much. She eats beautiful foods, artichokes, avocadoes, persimmons and pomegranates, wild rice with wild mushrooms, chrysanthemum tea. She doesn't have many possessions. Each thing is special. I wish you could see the way she arranged her treasures on the fireplace mantle. She has a splendid collection of cups, bowls, and baskets.

Well, the herbs are still in alphabetical order, and I can't complain about how the house looks. Since Intuition moved in, my life has been turned inside out.

Pain

Pain is subtle. He has cold grey fingers. His voice is hoarse from crying and screaming. Some people think any time they feel something they don't understand, it is Pain. Other people think feelings themselves are a sign of Pain. When people try to avoid him, he follows them silently and turns up as the bartender or the bus driver or the auctioneer. Pain has an elaborate filing system for keeping track of everyone; he is thinking about asking an old friend of mine to computerize it.

The local university wants to grant Pain tenure, but the students insist his teaching is overrated. The faculty is impressed because when Pain presents his work, it sounds meaningful and difficult.

Pain respects people who are willing to take risks. If you face him directly, he will give you a special ointment so your wounds don't fester.

Imagination

When Imagination walks, she writes letters to the earth. When she runs, her feet trace postcards to the sun. And when she dances, when she dances, she sends love letters to the stars.

Some people accuse Imagination of being a liar. They don't understand that she has her own ways of uncovering the truth. She studied journalism in junior high school. It gave her an excuse to leave school early and interview interesting people. She was surprisingly good at writing articles. When in doubt, she just made things up. More recently, Imagination has been working as a fortuneteller in the circus. She has this way of telling your fortune so clearly that you believe her, and then your wishes start to come true.

Imagination is studying photography now with an eye to making films. She has no intention of working in one of those factories where they manufacture images that lull us to sleep. Her vision is more complex, and very simple. Even with the old stories, she wants us to see what has never been seen before.

Jealousy

Jealousy stands by the blue flame of the gas stove stirring obsession stew. In his mind he is tearing people limb from limb. He wears a shirt that is almost in style with its odd angular shapes and bright edges. He can be quite charming when he wants to be. He certainly has a flair for drama. After a while, though, the roles Jealousy takes begin to seem shallow, dishonest, repetitive. The more upset he feels, the more loudly he denies it. For a time I stopped giving parties because he wouldn't come if I invited certain people. At that point I couldn't give a party without inviting him, and I was unwilling to censor my guest list for his sake. He is quite capable of showing up anywhere, unexpected, uninvited, unwelcome.

Terror

Terror is stricter than my first Latin teacher. She doesn't want anyone to become friendly with Ecstasy or run through the hills racing the Wind. On the west wall of her living room she keeps a long list of rules and a tally sheet of those she frightens and those who frighten her. In the margins she records your weaknesses. She demands privacy, but she doesn't hesitate to bother others at any hour of the day or night.

When Terror wants power, she has many ways to silence those who oppose her. She is willing to use violence to achieve her ends; often she prefers less obvious means. Terror knows that she can control the body by controlling the mind. When people are in states of confusion, Terror's propaganda passes for truth.

Terror came to our meditation class for a while. It was hard to breathe when she was in the room. However, she never stayed long. After a few minutes, she always opened her eyes. She knew if she sat really still she would scream.

Depression

Depression is the child of Lethargy and Despair. She was born tired. She has always had beautiful dreams. As she grew up, she stopped believing in them. The only person she could talk to then was Rage. He sat next to her during the geography class. When Rage left, Depression felt totally abandoned.

Depression sits at the table staring out the window as if there's no escape. She makes sure no one comes too close. Then she frets about being lonely. You warned me not to take her overtures of friendship too seriously. I wasn't paying attention. After all, I hardly have the time for my good friends, and I figured she would bore me. It wasn't until my neck was hurt that I found out why so many people want to spend time with her.

Greed

Greed is lonely and impulsive. He eats his food quickly and can't remember what it tastes like. He wants to make things stand still so he can understand, but he is always running somewhere himself. He was very cold as a child, and he still fears that he will never be warm enough.

Greed is a tyrannical boss. He needs a reason for everything. He used to disguise his temper with a thin layer of politeness. Since he has become rich and famous, he doesn't bother with amenities. He masks his fear of women with contempt. He exports nightmares on the international commodities market, an advertising executive turned pornographer of the soul.

Charm

Charm is very beautiful, and she is not afraid to wear her beauty on the outside. She works the late shift at the crisis center. She is a good counselor because she experiences her feelings completely. She has a way of offering solace that is subtle and light; she does not judge other people's craziness at all.

When Charm walks into the room, I sometimes hear the whisper of a silver flute following her. She delights in pretty clothes, soft colors and bold textures and skirts that whirl around her ankles and beautiful rings. Even when she had to wear a grey uniform, it was as if she were surrounded by butterflies and lilacs. Charm loves the sexual dance and the shimmering, shivering heat of erotic intensity, but when she says goodbye, she takes all of herself with her.

Charm does not understand the separation between work and play. She is certainly not lazy, but she needs to sing. You must remember that she is Inspiration's niece.

Competition

Competition is ruthless. He has to have an enemy. Otherwise, he has a "life is meaningless" crisis. For him there is only one right way, and it must be that way always. He has no respect for different colors, different crop varieties, or different points of view. He will divide life down to its smallest particle in his search to find the only best.

It is hard to say no to Competition. He makes the game sound so inviting until you are caught in the middle and begin to see how he has rigged it. He makes up all the rules and tells us some of them. We tried to change the game, and he kicked us out. Years later I dream I have forgotten to turn in the final assignment, and I am failing his class. His rules still haunt me.

Competition was in love with Creativity, but he married Efficiency. Not that Creativity would have married him. Competition and Efficiency seem more like allies than lovers. They never shout when they disagree. They settle their differences logically. However, it is not all as rational as it seems on the surface. Efficiency still feels more than a little jealous of her husband's passionate past. She has all kinds of plans and schemes to banish Creativity completely once she is secure in her position and certain of Competition's loyalty.

Luckily for us, no one is ever certain of Competition's loyalty. Considering his short attention span, history of treachery, and inability to ever make a commitment to anyone, we can almost assume Creativity will be safe from Efficiency's snares.

Defeat

Defeat sits in his chair staring at the grey doves on
the porch. He holds his hand underneath his heart,
fingers curled tightly into themselves, glued together
in a paralyzed rage. He is unwilling to go forward
and unable to let go. He is not blind or deaf, but it is
unclear who he sees or what he hears. He had a
stroke six years ago and sleeps most of the day. In
response to questions he answers yes or no inter-
changeably. Speech has lost all meaning.

Forgiveness

Forgiveness is a strong woman, tender and earthy and direct. Since her children have left home, she has embarked on an extended walking tour, visiting ruins and old monuments, bathing in rivers and hot springs, traveling through the small towns and large pulsing cities, tracing the current of sorrow under the stories she hears. Sometimes the city authorities and officials don't want her within their gates. If the people want her there enough, she always manages to find a way inside.

Forgiveness brings gifts wherever she goes. Simple ones, a three-stranded twig with leaves turning yellow, a belt she wove on an inkle loom, a little song that grows inside you and changes everything. She brought me a silver ring from the South with a pale stone, pink with a hint of brown. When I had asthma, she taught me how to breathe.

Commitment

Commitment has kind eyes. He wears sturdy shoes. Everything is very vivid when he is around. It is wonderful to sit and have lunch in his gardens around harvest time. You can taste in the vegetables that the soil has been cared for.

Because Commitment is so serious, he loves clowns and balloons and fools and limericks. He has four daughters, grown now, but when they were little they always took him to the circus.

There is something special about the way Commitment gazes at the new moon. I wish I knew how to explain it. He is such a simple man, and yet he is mysterious. He is more generous than most people. His heart is open. He is not afraid of life. He is married to Joy.

Whimsy

Whimsy is not afraid to be outrageous but she is basically shy. She has all kinds of books, and she arranges them on the shelves by the color of the cover or how the titles sound next to each other. She was especially pleased to put a book on African dyeing called *Into Indigo* next to a dark blue book on Jewish mysticism. Her clothes are also kept by color in the closet.

When Whimsy was a little girl, she would stay in the museum with the marble walls talking to the statues after everyone else left. She has trouble keeping her shoelaces tied but in every other way she is as practical as your next door neighbor. Because she is wild, people expect her to entertain them. She is not encouraging anyone else to live like her. Remembering how abruptly her brother was locked up for being a troublemaker, she fears people who treat her like a curiosity. Freedom is her lover.

Ecstasy

Ecstasy builds slow fires, but they burn for a long time. His eyes are the color of the clear summer night. He loves the drum and the flute and the dark winter moon. He knows many things, but he does not talk much. If you try to pin him down, he will answer you with music. You have to decide for yourself what he really means.

Ecstasy runs an inn for travelers high in the Turquoise Mountains. It is an interesting job because he is never quite sure who will turn up. There are no reservations here, and the meals are free. The mountain air brings clear dreams, and some of the guests start to settle in. Ecstasy insists that no one stay too long. He is running an inn, not a boarding house. He also leaves the inn from time to time.

The inn is not always easy to find. It is not on the main road, and sometimes the signs disappear. Don't attempt the journey if you are in a rush or are scared to be by yourself. Even Ecstasy loses his way if he has been gone for awhile.

Ecstasy was a jeweler before he came to these mountains. His jewelry has always been simple. The designs are completely right. His lines are true. He especially likes to work with amber and jade and diamonds. It was his search for crystals that first brought him to the Turquoise Mountains.

Liberation

Liberation tried to commit suicide when he was seventeen. Things got even worse before they got better. He was married to Terror for nearly ten years. One day when he was wandering famished and half-crazy in the mountains, he bumped into Ecstasy. Ecstasy wept to be reunited with his old friend and taught Liberation a simple prayer. After that Liberation was free to leave Terror.

Creativity

Creativity is not efficient. She has a different relationship to time than most of us. A minute can last a day and a day can last an hour. She loves all the seasons. She is on intimate terms with the sun and the moon. It is New Year's all year long at her house, what with celebrations for the Celtic, Hebrew, Tibetan, Chinese, Japanese, and other New Years too numerous to mention. Creativity loves to gossip with the birds and put on her masks and beads and dance with the animals. Although bright colors amuse her, she most often wears neutral tones. She is especially partial to off-white.

Some people consider Creativity selfish because she does what she wants. I have always found her to be gracious and most generous. She is certainly complex. If you have only met her in a serene mood, her flair for drama may offend you. She is not your aunt with the porcelain teapot who plays chamber music. If you are one of those people who only go to see her when she is starring in a major melodrama, you will not hear her rain songs. If you insist she is mad, you will never see how still her face is when she returns from a dream.

Sometimes Creativity disappears completely or wanders around the back alleys for weeks at a time. She has a strong need to be occasionally anonymous. If you run into her at the post office line during one of these periods, you will probably not recognize her. She is in a different place. It is almost as if her blood has slowed down. When the blank period is over, Creativity brings her free self home with her. Her skin is new. She is ready to work. More than anyone else, Creativity understands the secret meanings of the months when nothing seems to get done.

Honor

Many people would consider Honor a poor man. Of course, there were times when he was fabulously wealthy. For a while he lived in a large house with arches and courtyards and fountains and gardens and olive trees and rare birds. Now he lives in a tiny room with windows on three sides. He still likes to go out for breakfast on special occasions.

Honor has a different sense of value than most of us. When Honor was famous, all kinds of people came knocking on the door asking for favors. Since he has met with hard times, many of his old friends are afraid to be seen with him, as if hard times would notice and visit them too. This turn of events saddens Honor but he has never tried to change other people.

Honor is an old man now. He is becoming more transparent. He walks softly, and people do not hear him as he walks past them on his way to the park. Honor's children, impatient with his old-fashioned manners, complain about him to their friends. His grandchildren adore him. Only his childhood friend Humility has stayed loyal through the long rainy winter.

Certainty

Sometimes all the Qualities seem to talk at once, and I don't know who to listen to first. Certainty comes into the room and stands in the doorway and gives me a good long look until I hear the silence again.

When Certainty is bored, he disguises himself in old clothes and goes to the bars with Confusion. He has an outstanding sense of direction; he knows how to walk until everything makes sense again. When Creativity is lost inside his mind, he writes his name over and over until he is back.

Certainty knows many alphabets. He is an architect with language. His words build meanings. He loves fine calligraphy and beautiful type. He once told me, "My love affair with language goes down to the letter."

Although Certainty is an excellent scholar, he starts to miss the trees when he spends too much time with his books. He enjoys documenting his thoughts and investigating philosophical theories. In his own inimitable way he is trying to find out where ideas come from and how they grow.

Longing studies archeology. She is at home in the future as well as the past. She collects mirrors and antique necklaces. The lamps in her living room have embroidered shades, silk with beaded fringes. She takes long walks in the early autumn evening when everything looks dark green and purple and brown and deep blue, and the windows of the little houses shine yellow from the lights inside.

Longing speaks the language of dreams. She is a dancer and an actress. She knows tides and currents and pirates. She has swum in all the oceans, and traveled to places that the rest of us have only visited in our sleep.

Although I have met Longing many times, it is not easy to describe her appearance. She dresses herself with an awareness of where she is going and who will be there. It is more than the costumes though. Even the gossip columnist who notices everything could not quite remember Longing's height or the color of her sea-filled eyes. If you must see her, invite her to a concert. She is especially fond of the music of stringed instruments.

Intensity

Intensity's shirts are burgundy, and deep brown, and indigo. It's easy for him to forget about the paler tones. Sometimes, he seems to live as if the moon were always full; yet, he knows her dark side well. He rarely eats regular meals. He may be celibate for years at a time or spend weeks in bed with his beloved. He is very sensitive, and when he was younger, he worried about getting too close to people and driving them away. His family told him "not to feel things so much" and "not to try to change the world." Trying to follow their advice, he was sick and cynical. When he was scared to be himself, he was scary to be around. He is healthier now. I never cared much for his brooding pose but when he is well, no one is more handsome.

Intensity is a splendid actor. He pulls each part out of himself. He has tried on many roles in his attempt to discover who he is and why we suffer. He has traveled through the desert, chanting, praying, singing Hebrew love songs. For all his attraction to the unpredictable, there is a core of inner consistency. When he is calm, I am reminded of deep water on a quiet night. He is not as serious as he seems, and he needs friends who understand that. If he knows that you are serious, he will reveal his playful side to you. Just from knowing him I have learned so much. From time to time I want to give him back something tangible — a nourishing meal, bread for his next journey, or spring flowers in the lighter shades, the first yellow daffodils of February, the beautiful iris of early in April, purple veins outlining violet petals.

Integrity

Integrity takes long thoughtful walks. When she comes home, her pockets are full of stones and shells and feathers. She is the daughter of a weaver, and she has inherited her mother's sense of texture and color, though she prefers the potter's wheel to the loom. She makes ritual vessels for the local temple. It was through working with clay that Integrity grew to understand that the body is also a vessel, beautiful, sturdy, empty, and sacred.

Integrity loves the intersection where sculpture becomes dance. She has a supple spine and lovely muscles. She knows sign language and has often worked as an interpreter. When she speaks with her hands, it is not in grand, dramatic gestures but in soft, subtle movements. Watching her hands dance, we hear stories that we have no words for.

Complacency

Complacency has written lullabies and liturgies, also a lot of ad copy. She has a sweet voice and a gracious manner. The governor's wife, the perfect hostess, Complacency is not as apolitical as she seems. She has spent years learning how to apply her make-up and to camouflage the wrinkles on her forehead. Her mask is impenetrable now. Inside her breasts there are volcanoes smouldering. Do you think we can reach her before she explodes?

Anger

Anger sharpens kitchen knives at the local supermarket on the last Wednesday of the month. His face is scarred from adolescent battles. He has never been very popular. His reputation as a fighter dates back to seventh grade. Children never understand how Anger arrives at the house just in time for dinner. We never hear him ring the bell All of a sudden he is there. As soon as my son hears his footsteps, he is running for shelter underneath the twin bed in the guest room.

Anger is trying to gain Truth's friendship and respect. Anger is a meticulous reporter. He is accurate about details and insists on the facts. He never lies, but he rarely understands anyone else's point of view. It is true that sharp knives work better than dull knives; they are also safer. A cut from a dull knife takes a long time to heal. However, if you have not used a sharp blade for a while, it is easy to hurt yourself. If you must ask Anger to sharpen your bread knife, be careful how you handle it. He is not the only knife sharpener in town anymore.

Intelligence

Sometimes Intelligence is safe, and sometimes Intelligence is dangerous. When he is in a reassuring mood, you leave his house walking lightly and singing to yourself because everything makes sense. Other days you go to see him, and he tears up your notes or sends you back on the road even though you really want to stay home. If Intelligence is in the mood for facts, he may interrogate you for hours.

Intelligence does not go to parties much. He is very popular when he does show up. Everyone knows him, but no one knows where he will turn up. You may find him in the upstairs bedroom talking to the children or out on the back porch telling bad jokes. Intelligence listens well. He is no stranger to silence.

Intelligence is Intuition's favorite lover. It is thought that theirs is an attraction of opposites, but they are more similar than they first appear. Other people tried to keep them part for years by telling each of them vicious stories about the other. When you see them dance, it is clear they have been through the fire. They like to make up stories together.

Intelligence knows how to use words to make music and how to use words to make pictures. He thinks in black and white, but he dreams in color. Intelligence takes photographs with his inner eye. He paints with logic. Intelligence loves surprises, and he is not afraid to change his mind.

Boredom

Does anyone really know what Boredom is like? He rarely goes anywhere without at least one of his friends. He can't stand to be alone. On Sunday afternoons he goes to the bar on the corner and drinks dark beer with Futility, Rage, and Anxiety. They all have such strong personalities. In conversations with that bunch Boredom tends to get lost. It's not that he doesn't say anything. It is just that what he says never sounds as interesting or vivid or memorable. If you listen carefully, you will see that he actually has some very good ideas. He simply lacks the energy to carry them out.

Perseverance

Is there a school where Perseverance teaches classes? I want to meet him face to face and see what he looks like. I have heard so much about him. It is not that I want his feedback. I am sure he would tell me to "keep working," and I already know that. It is not just me either. Offhand, I can name at least three friends who are as curious as I am. One is a scholar, one is a writer, and the third is a young parent. I would write Perseverance a letter inviting him to come here and teach at the neighborhood school, but no one around here knows where he lives or how to find him.

I read somewhere that they were trying to hire him to co-host a PBS series on the creative process, but he would have none of it. Says he is shy in front of cameras. Truth is, he turns down all offers which distract him from his work.

Shock

Because Shock is difficult to get along with, his landlord tried to evict him, claiming that with Shock in the building none of the other tenants stayed for more than six months. The landlord found out soon enough it's not so easy to make Shock go away. I could have told him that.

Shock drove the ambulance after my accident. When I first came to, I told Shock this couldn't be happening to me. Not now. Not like this. Not out of the blue on a good day. When I woke again, I was in the hospital, and he was gone. I desperately wanted to ask him some questions. What happened? And why? I became obsessed with the details of the event. Now we've met several times through the years. Though we rarely speak of that morning, it changed our whole relationship.

Resignation

Greed and Resignation are to be married next month. Some people were surprised by this announcement. After all, Greed is much older than her. It seems strangely appropriate to me. Greed never listens to anyone else, and Resignation never says what she wants.

Resignation has many talents, but you would never know it from talking to her. She went to high school with my ex-husband. Thumbing through his old yearbook, I was shocked to see how beautiful she was, even then. She was popular and planned to go to law school.

In college Resignation took a part-time job selling tickets for one of Greed's commuter trains. Now she spends her time sitting at a desk and signing papers on the 38th floor. She is too vain to frown with her mouth. The expression in her eyes contradicts her smile.

Resignation would rather curse the darkness than light a candle. At first she intimidated me; now she infuriates me. I understand her too well. For a while we had similar taste in music, and I would run into her at concerts. It is no use talking to her about how strong or beautiful she is. She won't listen.

Resignation has an elegant neck which she hides behind melancholy collars and tall sweaters. Her throat is sore from the words she swallows. People close to her have been tortured, and she is afraid to speak out. When she meets someone she wants to please, she gives them a piece of her power wrapped up as if it were a jewel.

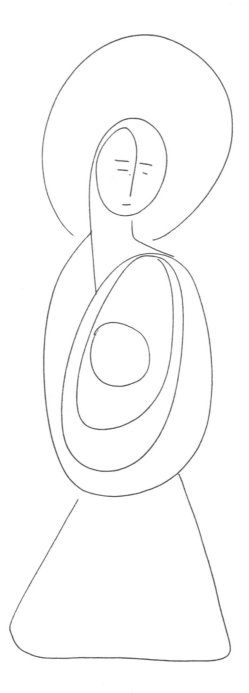

Protection

Protection is sensible and artistic. In this country we know her as a craftswoman. For her living she makes capes and weaves shawls. She has also been a midwife. She notices that some people insist on wearing her garments far into the hot season. Others refuse to put a cloak on even when they are cold.

Protection has lived in many kinds of houses. Always the walls are decorated with rugs and blankets from around the world. She has studied ancient architecture and the habits of butterflies and spiders. When the caterpillar is dying and the new butterfly is yet to be born, it constructs a chrysalis. We also have this need. However, many of us are too proud or have forgotten how to go inside. Protection has learned from the butterflies how to make a chrysalis for the changing human heart.

ambivalence

I remember one evening when Ambivalence and I sat down to enjoy a nice dinner on the porch. The phone rang, and he jumped out of his chair to answer it. When he came back to join me at the table, the soup was cold, and his mind was preoccupied with programming details. It was useless trying to talk to him. The only way I could gain his attention was to make a scene. Before I realized it, we were once again engaged in a power struggle, and my irritation gave him the advantage. He was clear that it was only my problem that I needed consistency, and added that the soup tastes best when it's lukewarm.

As you know, the relationship went on like that for years. As soon as I would start to organize my life without him, beautiful love letters appeared in my mailbox. When I grew fond of our weekends in the country, he became indifferent. It took me a long time to figure out that for him indecision is a desired form of suspense. This game of yes/no/maybe intrigues him. It left me exhausted, and I can see that it is beginning to give you a nervous stomach.

Panic

Panic has thick curly hair and large frightened eyes. She has worked on too many projects meeting other people's deadlines. She thinks she has an incurable disease. No one else has been able to confirm or deny it. She wakes up in the middle of the night pulling her hair out. She wants to dig underneath her skin and pull this illness out by its roots. She grabs at her scalp instead. She is crying for help, but only when she is sure no one is around to hear her.

Panic drives recklessly. She speeds down the freeway in an attempt to outrace her fears and numb her nerves. As she rushes to the city, she mutters about the accidents and the traffic and the isolation of each driver safely locked inside a little machine. Her anger at the distant politicians is mixed up with her confusion about how to make her own life mean something. We are all out of control, pretending to be in control.

Panic is sure no one can help her. She insists that she must sweat out these demons on her own. Although people care about her, she refuses to see them. She is ignoring the evidence of her own senses. When she is held, she is healed. Like the politicians she despises, she is scared to be touched.

Truth

Truth is tall and rather unconventional looking. He has golden hair and a short beard. He does not like statistics and is not particularly concerned about facts, but he loves a good story. He chronicled the contemporary film scene for a while. He quit when his reviews started being quoted out of context. Though he never hides what he feels, by nature he is gentle and not at all sarcastic. However, he does have a fierce temper. He has observed that people who only listen with one ear when he says something in a kind way are always impressed by his anger.

Truth has been employed as a thief stealing illusions. He can climb over any security fence we have constructed to keep out disturbing influences. Although he can unlock any window or door, he is no longer interested in breaking in or getting away. No longer thrilled by the chase nor by defying authorities, he has given up on the challenge of trying to find new ways to escape.

X-rays, photographs of cells, and the history of plants fascinate Truth. When Truth's fingers touch my shoulder, I hear bone touching bone. Truth has set down his bundle of needs, and his shoulders are soft and spacious, outlined by light.

Truth learned to act in the theater of qualities, and his studies in mime continue. He lingers in the long pauses between the questions and the answers. He has made an altar to his loneliness. Certainty and Uncertainty are both welcome at his table. Truth is willing to wait for a long time with little attention or visible encouragement. Truth is not willing to live without Love.

Service

Service is Devotion's practical sister. She is a funny one, sort of austere and sensuous at the same time. She isn't as stern as she was as a young child, and she is not in such a hurry but her intensity has not diminished at all. She has learned that seeds must be watered before they sprout. Some lie dormant for years. Shoots must be nurtured before they bloom. We all work in different ways.

Sometimes we need to remind Service to take a vacation. She sees so much that needs to be done, and she forgets that she also needs to rest. In my opinion, Service would be a marvelous job counselor — if you can imagine the Employment Development Department hiring someone like her. She never asks you to do what you cannot do, but only what you most truly can do.

Alienation

When I first called Alienation to arrange an interview, he said he couldn't do it right now. "Everything is poisoned. Our speech is the language of captives. All attempts to communicate are futile or pretentious."

At that point I called around to find out more about his life story. It seems that he was a delightful child, curious and playful, and gentle. He was popular in art school and began his career sculpting massive figures. Although his work was praised, he could not reach the people he honored. Their indifference chilled him. He was hungry and frustrated, and his work became brutal and inaccessible. After his daughter was born, he gave up his studio and took a job downtown to support his family. He is very good at what he does, but it means nothing.

Alienation's associates are worried that he is really going crazy now. They miss the accuracy and insight of his sarcastic comments. As usual, he could say, "No one understands me." This time he doesn't care. He needs to be left alone. He is tearing off his masks. He is exploring the layers underneath the language of lies. He is in a labyrinth, and he is searching for Compassion. Though he hasn't found her yet, he sees the signs of her presence. He is recovering the pieces of his childhood self.

If you have an opportunity to talk with Alienation, don't lie to him or attempt to justify your compromises. Listen carefully. He is honest with himself. He will penetrate your mask.

Blame

Blame keeps a pharmacist's scale at the corner of his desk. He is very good at measuring emotions and calculating who has suffered more than whom. No one doubts that he is clever.

I shared my bed with Blame for nearly three years. I trusted him initially because he was eloquent. Whenever we fought, his words seemed clear and logical. I assumed his was the more valid point of view. It took me years to catch on to his methods. He had this way of taking my position and exaggerating it until I felt ridiculous.

Blame is not honest. I saw him for lunch last Friday. He confessed that he was puzzled because he keeps running into the same problems in all his relationships. He insists that he admires and respects strong women. Maybe he does . . . in the abstract. When he is in relationship with one, he is intent on subverting her power.

Unhappiness

Well, your children told me Unhappiness has volunteered to cook for you. I understand you do not enjoy fixing meals for your hungry household. Still, I must warn you to consider this offer carefully. Unhappiness was the cook in my dormitory food service years ago. Her favorite meal is burnt lentils with stale toast. Her taste in vegetables runs toward the rotten. Even when she makes foods that taste good, you leave the table vague and unsatisfied; you find yourself eating flat bread in the corner of the pantry an hour later. Complaining to her about the food does not help. Mean comments please her. Just because Unhappiness thrives on misfortune and blackened bread, doesn't mean they will nourish you.

Ugliness

Ugliness is a thief screaming, "I have been denied, I have been denied, I have been denied." She is trying to steal back the sense of belonging which was stolen from her when she was younger. If you fear that she wants to take your beauty, you are right. She does. If you try to stop her, she will find another way to get you. It is a vicious cycle. If you offer her the bracelet she was eyeing, she will smash it out of shape. She believes anything that comes to her easily must be worthless.

Ugliness has excellent eyes but dull vision. She believes that she has unhealthy hair and bad skin and a weird body. However, she has no idea what she really looks like. She spits at mirrors. She insists that if you are attractive, people will notice, and then they will try to possess you. They will break you apart, consume you, and throw you away. Ugliness spends more time than she'd admit making sure that she doesn't look good. She is so busy not pleasing anyone else that she is never free to be herself. Hurt, Ugliness has decided it is better to steal rather than risk being ripped off again.

Devotion

Devotion lights candles at dusk. She braids her grandmother's hair with an antique comb. She works as an ecologist at the university. She wears long flowing tunics with bright cotton pants. She has never taken a dance class, but she moves with an unstudied grace, sensitive to the edge where her body meets the air.

Devotion balances periods of great stillness with times of movement and exuberance. She has prayed in many temples and seen evidence of God in unlikely places. She keeps a postcard of Saint Francis above her desk. A Yemenite amulet hangs in her window. Always she remembers to honor the Mother.

Inspiration

Inspiration is disturbing. She does not believe in guarantees or insurance or strict schedules. She is not interested in how well you write your grant proposal or what you do for a living or why you are too busy to see her. She will be there when you need her but you have to take it on trust. Surrender. She knows when you need her better than you do.

Urgency

Urgency has the beard of a Hebrew prophet and the eyes of a medieval alchemist. He reads history books in the middle of the night. He stands behind me when I am at the typewriter. He is brilliant, and his thoughts leap across great startling distances, but he expects me to go back and fill in the missing pieces. He is impatient with my tendency to avoid strenuous exercise.

Urgency hates to be late. He runs up the stairs racing the escalator. He works for a messenger service on weekends. He is always on the lookout for allies. If Urgency thinks you may be able to help him, he will sit you down and ask you for your life story. First, he wants to find out what motivates you, and then, he listens for what fascinates you.

Honesty

Honesty is the most vulnerable man I have ever met. He is simple and loving. He lives in a small town on a cliff near the beach. I had forgotten how many stars there are in the midnight sky until I spent a week with him at his house by the sea.

In my time I have been afraid of so many things, most especially of the heights and of the darkness. I know if I had been driving anywhere else, the road would have terrified me. Knowing I was on my way to see him softened the fear. And in his presence the darkness becomes big and deep and comforting. He says if you are totally vulnerable, you cannot be hurt.

Grief

Before she came to this town Grief was a woman named Eliea. She was a potter, and she glazed her big-bellied pots with earth colors until they shone like dull bronze. She had four children. The daughters live inland now in the distant foothills, and the oldest son left the family as soon as he could get away. It was the young boy with the golden curls and the laughing eyes who gave her great joy. He loved the ocean. He was barely walking when he learned to swim and not much older when he started to sail. One day about two years ago the sailors brought his boat home empty.

Never have I heard such sounds of weeping as when Grief found out her son had drowned. She screamed and howled. She stamped her feet and smashed her pots and bowls. She ate with all her fingers. She tore at her hair, and it grew wild and matted. She wandered from place to place with no sense of where she was or how she came there.

One day at the edge of the forest Grief heard another woman crying out. She spoke with her. She listened to her story. Grief was surprised. She had never met anyone else who had suffered as she had. Together the women sat in the clearing and mourned their children. Through the long afternoon, through the twilight, through the night, they wept and wept and wept and wept. In the morning Grief was washed clean of her tears. She came to our town and started to do her real work.

Sensuality

Sensuality does not wear a watch but she always gets to the essential places on time. She is adventurous and not particularly quiet. She was reprimanded in grade school because she couldn't sit still all day long. She needs to move. She thinks with her body. Even when she goes to the library to read Emily Dickinson or Emily Bronte, she starts reading out loud and swaying with the words, and before she can figure out what is happening, she is asked to leave. As you might expect, she is a disaster at office jobs.

Sensuality has exquisite skin and she appreciates it in others as well. There are other people whose skin is soft and clear and healthy but something about Sensuality's skin announces that she is alive. When the sun bursts forth in May, Sensuality likes to take off her shirt and feel the sweet warmth of the sun's rays brush across her shoulder. This is not intended as a provocative gesture but other people are, as usual, upset. Sensuality does not understand why everyone else is so disturbed by her. As a young girl, she was often scolded for going barefoot.

Sensuality likes to make love at the border where time and space change places. When she is considering a potential lover, she takes him to the ocean and watches. Does he dance with the waves? Does he tell her about the time he slept on the beach when he was seventeen and woke up in the middle of the night to look at the moon? Does he laugh and cry and notice how big the sky is?

It is spring now, and Sensuality is very much in love these days. Her new friend is very sweet. Climbing into bed the first time, he confessed he was a little intimidated about making love with her. Sensuality just laughed and said, "But we've been making love for days."

Harmony

Harmony doesn't seem extraordinary until you have known him for a while. He knows how to be gentle, and such gentleness is surprisingly powerful. The silence around him is lyrical. If I sit in his kitchen in the late afternoon and drink ginger tea, by the time I am ready to go home the contradictions inside my head are no longer shouting at me and trying to tear each other apart. He gives me space to be my whole self.

It may be hard to believe it now, but there was a time when Harmony was afraid to leave his house. I am not sure about the whole story. In college he was an outstanding athlete, and he won many prizes. One summer when he was training intensively, he became dissatisfied with the whole set-up. Torn apart inside, he could no longer keep his balance. He alienated many of his friends with his tirades about hypocrisy and ugliness. Frustrated with people, he took long walks through the neighboring countryside. He found sanity in the geometry of the old buildings and started dreaming about how to organize spaces in which he could feel more comfortable, thus, stumbling into the profession of architecture through a back door. He has learned how to design rooms which evoke different aspects of our selves. Although he is a meticulous architect, he is no longer fussy and alienated. He can go anywhere now. Simply by being himself, he alters the current in the field around him.

Joy

Joy drinks pure water. She has sat with the dying and attended many births She denies nothing. She is in love with life, all of it, the sun and the rain and the rainbow. She rides horses at Half Moon Bay under the October moon. She climbs mountains. She sings in the hills. She jumps from the hot spring to the cold stream without hesitation.

Although Joy is spontaneous, she is immensely patient. She does not need to rush. She knows that there are obstacles on every path and that every moment is the perfect moment. She is not concerned with success or failure or how to make things permanent.

At times Joy is elusive — she seems to disappear even as we approach her. I see her standing on a ridge covered with oak trees, and suddenly the distance between us feels enormous. I am overwhelmed and wonder if the effort to reach her is worth it. Yet, she waits for us. Her desire to walk with us is as great as our longing to accompany her.

Acknowledgements

The hermit in me often tries to overshadow my more social aspect. For all my attempts to make a religion of solitude, I am amazed how much I need and enjoy and love the people who have touched me and changed my life.

During the process of writing the Qualities I have felt especially blessed by the presence of good friends. I want to thank Marian O'Brien for her vision and ability to bring visual ideas into finished form, Rosemary Warden for her creative spirit, and Debra Ann Robinson for arranging the first reading and massaging away my doubts. Selene Kumin Vega saw the original Qualities and knew there was a book waiting long before I could see it. Clive Matson, Jonathan Tenney, and Kymberley Moses independently and simultaneously reminded me to attend to my writing. For feedback, encouragement, and support I acknowledge: Kate Dodge, Sharon Elliot, Beth Gendler, Jeremy Griffith, Malcolm Margolin, Tasha Marshe, Cedrus Monte, Annie Moose, Linda Sanford, Georgia Schwimmer, Judith Schulz, Charlie Werner, Keith Whitaker, Lawrence Whitehead, Jim Williams. Special thanks to Barbara Juhasz for long distance perspective.

Both my parents have encouraged my love of stories. My mother spent many hours reading to us as we grew up. I still don't understand how my father had the patience to read the same story to an insistent three year old every night for a year. His wit and fondness for peopling the dinner table with imaginary characters who had funny names has more to do with all of this than I can know.

In the last few years there have been several important teachers. I especially want to thank Frank Doran and Vicki Noble. Elaine Chernoff's striking clarity has enabled me to commit myself more fully to my work. Finally, Gioia Timpanelli and Sandy Diamond each in her own way opened my eyes to the ways words dance.

Photo by Irene Young

Janet Ruth Gendler wears orange socks, arranges her clothes by color in the closet, keeps the herbs in alphabetical order, and doesn't understand the separation between work and play. Gendler was born and raised in Omaha, Nebraska and received B.A.'s in English and Communications from Stanford University in 1977. She has written articles on the arts, health, and education. She works in publishing and teaches intuitive art classes. Gendler currently lives in Berkeley, California.